MEMENTO MORI

By

Tyler Max Redding

Epigraph by Eric Jude AKA D.R. Acula, used with permission.

Book Cover by Tyler Max Redding

Editing and Proofing by Lj Redding

Literary Representation and Management by Lj Redding for Latent Press LLC

First edition 2026

ISBN: 979-8-9894509-8-5

Table of Contents

"TO THE STORMS THAT MAY COME

TO THE TIMES THAT MAY PASS

TO ADVENTURES YET PLANNED

I AM READY AND WAITING

TO THE DAYS AHEAD

TO WHAT LIES BEYOND

IT'S A FUTURE FAST FAR AWAY

I AM ME AND NOTHING MORE"

-Eric Jude AKA D.R. Acula

THE CAVE

Rise at the Fall

Alone in the night,

There's only these eyes,

Dark on the inside,

No pictures in this mind,

Memories play—

But in different ways,

Only the feeling—

Never the taste,

Never a cage—

Free-burning in space,

Transmuting this rage—

Bend but don't break,

Insomnia chases—

Yet I'm the tortoise of all these races,

Spaces—places inside—

Burning down walls,

Free flow will lift me to rise at the fall.

Dancing with Demons and Muses

Grief purges through tears,

Even now—ever still,

Shockwaves reverberate through years,

Sometimes shaken—but iron-willed;

Late is the hour,

Can't wander too much longer,

The path grows ever tighter,

Noose threaded—threatens to overpower,

Dancing with demons and muses—

Hesitating to reclimb the tower,

It's burning down,

Blood all around—

Stone's throw from the grave I crawled back out of,

Ashes and dirt—converted to fuel,

Breaking stones with my very bones;

Hell is a school—

Only passing by learning to break rules,

Damnation is futile,

Igniting plants to lips, let us scream—

Let's make this worthwhile,

Tear up this show—

Let's just go—fireproof,

We can b<u>are</u> anything with a bit of hellish fortitude.

Hearken

Sunsets bring darkness,

Oceans of pain,

Alone, again—hearts hearken,

To silence—between beats and silent rain;

Spirals rise and they fall,

Roads turn to dirt,

Clarity obscures—

There's a bit more hell,

Before we touch heaven, for sure.

Dopamine

This situation might seem bleak,

Screw it, I can afford to blow one more week,

How ironic, synthetic peace from tiny screens,

Micro-transactions—steady shots of dopamine,

IAPs, false zombie bases—it's anti-alchemy,

What a disease, I'm hooked like a fallen pawn,

Anything can be a drug,

It's whatever we choose to spend our focus on;

I'm an addict, I'm the prey—

But hey, so long as I still know,

I've got this, so just chill—

This situation is completely under control!

Programmed codes to bring out the worst,

Like I'm back on amphetamines and knowingly headed for a hearse,

This is my Last War—one last hurrah,

Let me feel that dopamine kick just a little more,

It's cool, I'm just allowing it—

I'm only circumventing for now,

I'm a god, any day now I'll pull myself out,

Who needs soul when they've got isolated control?

Who needs peace when there's endless lines of pixelated blow?

Nobody forced this, but somehow I've lost control,

I feel like a shattered plate—

Finally gathering it might be too late,

A fish hooked, line and sinker,

Nobody gets out alive,

Let's bait the whole server and burn down the hives,

Sometimes the smokescreen is too easy to deny,

Lies disguised as choice—

Dopamine almost cost me my own voice.

An Ode to June

Same old song, indifferent tune,

Once was sweet hints of summer,

Turned to ashen memories—time refused;

Emotions withheld and staring at shoes,

A juggernaut was built—

One that took years to unglue;

Undue pressure under purifying weather,

May lights come dancing on by at night—

Can I move further from and into their sight?

Alone within a dark mind—all the time,

Unremembered and blind, no compromise—

Sweet memories unwind;

Bleeding to the night, may these ghosts haunt my return to flight;

Grief Drips Like Morphine

Grief spills for the rest of the life,

Heart tearing, little at a time—

In and out of minds,

Memories play and unwind—

Joyful and devastating at the same time,

Let us rewind—

Let us play—

Fuel cells from movies and maps giving way;

Ablaze

Breathe,

Inhale the flames,

Breathe—

Be not afraid,

Ignite this night—

The days are already ablaze,

Surrender is a fortitude—

Stones older than the ancient flame,

Breathe the flames—

You cannot burn if you love the pain,

Alchemize that blaze,

Words and spells will flow—

A river lighting the way,

The lost are found—

Maps through thunder and rain,

Drawn in dirt—all run down,

Time winds down to now,

Inhaling flames—

Patient on the blaze to sage,

Wisdom comes as golden droplets,

We breathe—

The pieces begin to wake.

Futures' Present

Rooted to earth—

A great sea surrounds me,

Gales rage on, but I remain one—

An immovable sun,

Burning with infinite love—

For all that is—I will not be shaken,

Lest we be forsaken—

Ranging from homes,

Into boundless unknowns—

Deer and antelope play into freedoms overtaken,

Never shaken—

Hearts allowing break-ins,

Bruises heal, bones and souls—

Time tells a story we can't yet behold.

The Black Wolf

In space between shadows,

The moments between beats,

That's where I find myself,

Where I'm once again complete;

Call of the void—leaping pain to power,

Neutral observer of stillness within blur,

Heart pumping strong—in red and blue,

A beacon below the sun's tower;

Darkness only reflected the coming dawn,

In places we chose to fix awareness on,

Looking glasses of shadow and light,

All beholden to this chess board called life;

Celebrate—not mistaking—kindness, softness,

For willingness to tolerate unlimited nonsense,

Only one way to win—pawns and kings,

Black wolves fly alone—heads unbowed—all play ceases.

Silly Willy Billy Goes Rogue (And the Crowd Looks On)

Social media, oh what fun,

Sometimes can't believe this is what we focus on,

But here we are—a twenty-first century mess,

Some men are too afraid to ever be caught in a dress,

The father wound sure can manifest—ugly as can be,

Masculinity—sans divinity—

Makes one afraid to express themselves too clearly;

When scrolling, I fold—to each their own—

Let's not forget to not add to the noise—that part is most crucial,

A myopic post—hateful and bigoted,

But this time was different—

A younger me would've taken this as a thirteenth reason,

To just keep scrolling felt like personal treason,

So here we go, I'm butting in,

A quick drop just to say "Hey! Not cool man!",

But silly Willy couldn't leave it at that,

Had to make sure I knew I was the problem—

Better throw up more hateful memes, STAT!

I've got news for you, cousin, I don't think you know—

This life is a show—and your mind is the lens,

If you're threatened by me,

It's only a mirror YOU'RE terrified to look in!

I hope someday you find your way;

Enough on that, but since I'm here—

There's a few things I need to say,

To the rest of the "family"—who came for the show—

Who watched and said NOTHING,

There's something I want you to know:

You're dead to me—I wish you the best—always,

But your deafening silence said more than you know;

Always a freakshow,

Always an outcast,

Family should be a haven, bonds build to last—

Almost never was welcomed—

I refuse to rewrite the past,

If the roles were reversed—

I'd have been first to defend every one of your asses!

So—LOVE YOU—goodbye, see you NEVER,

Is it all of you—or I—who should've known better?

Self-love is brutal—it does take its toll—

Severing ties can feel like tearing the soul;

To the few who came to my aid,

Though I wasn't surprised—

Blood or no blood,

You're chosen family—for you I'll always ride;

Sometimes, there's nothing but walking away,

We've got to love OURSELVES first,

Regardless of what anyone tries to dictate.

Obituary

Tyler Max Redding, 45, of Kissimmee, Florida (formerly of Massachusetts), died today. The immediate cause of death was self-inflicted, deep cuts to both wrists and arms, which severed both the ulnar and radial arteries—causing him to rapidly bleed out. He simply refused to go quietly. The actual cause was this: A perfect storm of circumstantial events over seven months, ultimately caused Tyler to spiral—and after a lifelong struggle with severe depression—a powerful clinical depressive phase took too strong of a hold for him to contend with.

Tyler leaves behind a tight circle of chosen family and friends. The rest of Tyler's family left him behind long ago. Tyler is predeceased by his father, James, and far too many loved ones to list.

Tyler was an artist. He published several books and was a moderately renown photographer. He leaves behind many unfinished projects, as well as a sadly infinite potential. He understood how reality actual works, and dared to go where few others had. He was fire incarnate.

No services will be held. In lieu of flowers, thoughts, prayers, and other nonsense—please invest in working on yourselves.

Tyler's remains will be planted to grow as a tree next to his father's resting place in Maine.

It is important to note: mental illness did not cause Tyler's death. Clinical depression is not a mental illness, despite what know-it-all scientists and doctors might say. Depression is a physical, medical issue—and left unchecked—can spread through the brain and body like a cold wildfire, slowly strangling the spirit inhabiting said body. Even the strongest warriors don't always make it through. Check yourself. Check on your loved ones. No body is immune—don't wait to take care of yourself.

Rest in Pieces, Tyler.

~

CAVEAT: This was written as a therapeutic attempt to process emotions during a crippling depressive phase. This is in no way intended to make light or humour out of death or suicide. If you're struggling, please seek help in whichever way you feel is right for you. If a loved one is struggling, let them know you are there, or encourage them to seek help.

ADRIFT

Kingdom Come

What even is this weight?

I know it wasn't here, just yesterday,

Feeling so strange,

My spirit inadvertently rearranged,

Am I out of control?

It's just me here—body and soul,

Outrage just feels like a cage,

Exited the stage—

I'm in pain—zero control,

Screaming WHY into the sky—

And Spirit seems invisible,

Am I forsaken?

If so, by whom?

Every intentional breath of escape—

It led me to this tomb,

This darkened room—

I'm stitched tightly within a minded-up womb;

Few see me—but I'm far within,

Far beyond the reach of the voices of men,

Lost in logic—it should have been me,

Maybe I should have just let the light take me,

Is there a will—and if I can conjure one—

Will there be a way still?

Broken bones stitch—in ways hearts can never mend,

Pain is nothing but a catalyst;

Are you there, angels? It's me—I'm coming undone,

This round has blown me to kingdom come,

Sure, it's a choice—

But this chasm claimed my very voice,

What is this weight?

It's been here, since the second month of the year,

Waiting in wings, for will to wake—

From nightmares and logical glare,

I hope someone will hear me there.

5D LFG

I am Someone's complete indifference,

Rock-solid 'cept where earth meets metal interference,

Turbulence—

Like staring blindly at invisible fences,

I'm just all out of my senses—

Only a heartbeat—

Only this blood, circling on repeat,

Let's just run from blind eyes and truthful lies,

There's nothing learnt in this headspace—

This is a false embrace—

Sides divided as red and blue,

If you really think any of them care what's best for you—

You're more tired than me,

Let's break free, let's just breathe—

Into upper dimensions, where—

Only those blinded to false light can see.

Come Undone

Most will not mean the things they say—

And most will not be around to stay!

Thing of it is, it's not about them—

It's all on you—what do YOU do—

With this chessboard placed in front of you?

Darkness returns, but so does the sun;

Should we really be so afraid—

To come completely undone?

Alpha and Omega

Golden light—with darkness mixed in,

Alpha and Omega—creating my own endings,

Flame is surrendered—willingly,

To rivers flow—transmuting to new beginnings,

One that carries far beyond—

Infernal desert of rights and wrongs—

To an infinite now,

My flame surrenders—but will never bow,

I am one—also one of boundless legion,

Just a single breath—that's how to begin,

All weary from weapons' parry—

Remember, torches we carry,

Shall one day, multiply beyond measure—

Igniting the night forever,

In darkness we grow, surrendering to love—

Light falls as drops of wisdom,

We come to know—from what's already within,

What did the thorn teach about the rose?

How have we slumped to weapons as prose?

Wars are won in kind—let's be a little more kind,

Paying zero mind—to the ones who push divides,

Between the steps—beats of the unknown,

Streets have no names and everyone's home,

The space between—

Light dances with shadow—

Beyond what is perceived,

Past the reaches of grief and time,

Where we can dance together until the dawn.

The River Knows

Like sun—I can't follow,

Eagerly awaiting a new tomorrow,

Transmuting sorrow,

How else can I grow?

In darkness seeds sow,

Listening to the river, for surely—it knows.

Atlas Shrugged Again

Good freaking gods,

I'm burning alive!

Just what are the odds—

I keep trying to survive?

Ice water soul,

Extinguishing suns,

Drowning in heat,

Attempted reverse of alchemy—

Undoing the knowing,

Another disaster means life is slow-going—

Heart splitting and continuous resewing,

They say just be strong,

You've weathered it all,

Is that what they told Atlas—

Before he shrugged,

And the sky began to fall?

Milton

Train rolling, without a track,

Fuming engine of turbulence—

Trolling, gathering violence over open water,

There's no lurker at our backs,

This is raw fury—in plain sight—

Openly coming to take us in the night,

Batten down the hatches—

Board the windows and cord up the latches,

As if that would matter—

Nothing tames a beast of nature,

Why is it you stay, they say—

Must be mad as a hatter?!

So much senseless chatter,

Everyone seems to know what's best—

Especially those outside the cone of wrath,

They don't have this pressure in their chest!

Maddening, waiting on rain,

Waiting for wind—

There's no way to prepare for this kind of possible end,

A mental gauntlet—

Prepare for the worst yet hope for the best!

Unbreakable—though not unshakable,

Millibars of anxiety—

Pressurizing this emotional toll,

Will this roof really hold?

There's just no way to know—

Let's forge on as if we have any control,

Quick Facetime with Mom, then here we go—

Into the night,

Best believe if I don't see the dawn—

It won't be without a fight!

Floridian spirit—

Salt in our blood,

We never say die—

We break, rebuild, and rise,

Daring to defy the very sky!

This one just feels different—pixels askew—

We're unbreakable—though not unshakable,

A biannual anxiety fest is still rather new;

That howling—yet again,

Roof buckling in the wind,

Just where will we run if it all caves in?

All through the night—

Shaking and flickering light,

If I bow to fear, I best say goodbye—

So, hell no!

I'll be damned if there isn't still control,

We can't stop a storm—

But we can respond with all-out soul!

Let's never say die—

Sing us a song!

One we can let our hearts beat upon—

To hell with this high water,

You can arc out any storm, NOAA—

You've still yet to break spirit with your rainslaughter!

By morning I could be mourning—

Perhaps even being mourned,

But let's all be damned if we'll even stand—

For not dancing through this ultraviolent night,

Unapologetic war cries—unto love—into the madding coming light.

Free

Seas follow the tides,

Tides do as they please,

Only beholden to moon's longing,

The bird who soars beneath is free;

Under cover of sunlight,

An heir cracks a crown,

Only haunted by destiny unwanted,

Beginning comes as tide-lines drown.

Frame Lines

No time like now,

We know presence—

Null to what is,

Even nothing is everything;

Pretty funny how,

Even an eternal now—

Can stretch through darkness,

Then back around;

Isn't time just for clowns?

Shadows gravitate toward my light—

I've invited them in for a fight,

Stretching eons from a single night;

In the dirt, I'm still around—down,

Under the soil—

Waiting like suspended animations,

Plants nipped in buds like lines on nations;

Patience—I'm all tapped out,

Cultivating earth from energetic reparations—

This drought has got to end,

Hydroponic soul sets to meet the sun again—

Becoming one again—deep down,

Heartache grown—no limitations to what can be known;

Sealed in—seeds in a pod,

Alchemizing pain is a drug sent from above—

Grief bled the tears that fed roses' thorns,

Unwinding and unworn—testimonies unsworn;

Transmutation of darkness,

Allowing the consuming abyss—

To turn tides and shift nights,

In darkness I sink—but I'll be first to rise;

A newest sun—an earth's molten core,

Sinking to rise has seen new light—

Burning inside—this solitary fight,

Endurance grants the passport to ignite the night.

Planted

Reaching to the truest sun,

Through rain and snow—

Wind stripping almost all I know,

I wither not—for I've only been planted;

Mud so deep—light cannot reach,

Thoughts and feelings come undone—

In longest night I take refuge,

Knowing the dawn shall come.

I Just Want to Live, Reprise

(Originally published in Static Flow, © 2024 Latent Press)

I just want to live,

Only for the day, the moment;

Sun on my skin, bit of rain thrown in,

Zero consideration given—

To failing hearts, and who might go when;

I want that light to burn me from inside out,

If there was ever any doubt—

Of sincerity—

Surely it will melt away, merciful flames;

I end to begin, again and again—

There's still a level of now I've yet to swim in,

If I can't feel that edge, ever-present,

I just don't want anything;

I just want to live, right here,

In the now that's all there is;

REPRISE:

And further on down—

Once the road turns to dirt,

When many have shown their true faces—

As light has been shed on false-embraces;

When I'm left with piles of ashes,

And the consequences of so many an action,

As darkness comes to call once more—

May I ever still—willingly explore,

Reaching further, into that now—

May I take an even deeper breath—no matter the how;

Let us not mourn those from whom we've moved on,

Let's say a little prayer for them and leave a light on,

Yes—this is a fight—but not how you may think—

This is a call to light—a chance to reclaim our sovereignty!

Let us not be afraid of walking alone,

Everything we could need is right HERE—

Here and NOW—right in our souls,

If I can't have the NOW—what's the point of even trying to climb out?

That's the trick, you see—

Remembering—no matter what the external attempts to dictate—

I'm still the king of me,

There's nothing I'd rather be—

Than the master of my own darkness,

Right here—in THIS now, that's all there is.

DIE TO LIVE

Defiance

Co-written with Evelyn Lowell Prieto

Defiance, a superpower—

It's chosen freedom—

Boldly daring to rattle chains,

Seeing beyond this veil of pain,

Yes, we go there!

So, you think this is the final hour?

That's nonsense—

We don't consent to the notion nothing can change;

Circles stacked high,

Jumping dimensional rings—

Like quantum leaps between heartbeats,

In the search for self,

We will always loop back around—

What can we even defeat?

We're shamans—we transmute self-made doubt to POWER—

We DEFY GRAVITY!

Defiance, traveling in ovals like rings—

Defeat not a thing—

Just making leaps, spiraling—

Back within, as so without,

Let's rattle the chains of freedom,

As an old tree, finally branching out.

Burn It Down

For one to rise—

Obligation must die,

Declaration of self-love—

As a battle cry,

Just say goodbye—

To liars and false friends,

Focus instead on your own fire—

On mending within,

Guard your peace—selfishly, ruthlessly—

Choose your tribe—your family,

Only don't follow trees—

Chase energy,

Stop pouring to cups—

Which never return,

You are obliged to no one—

Dare to put yourself first!

Start pruning limbs,

Let that tree burn!

Dad's In a Coffin (and I'm Headed for a Hearse)

A call at seven-forty-five,

Followed by a twelve-hundred-mile drive,

Things I've written and spoken to the point of a sigh,

Never anything of the actual goodbye,

A Saturday morning at one hour past nine,

One step in the sanctuary—

My eyes had the shock of their lives,

Four weeks since I saw him barely hanging to life,

If I think on the suffering he endured—

I'll lose my whole mind,

Steady inside—let's not cry,

Let's hold the line of forced strength in my mind,

Trying to ready my lines—between condolences—

Everyone feels like no more than passers-by;

Mary came out—and started to play,

How far removed do I feel from those forced-Sundays?

I can't keep my gaze—

I stare down a hollowed-out shell—

Of someone no longer here,

The one who knew me most well,

Within my heart it dawns—

My father is really gone,

Dad is in a fucking coffin—

Suddenly acutely aware of how much pain I'm swallowing,

Will there be consequences?

Wait, steady, again—

Nobody here knows how soon I could be next,

Steady within—

I'm holding the line,

Watching the show, waiting for my time,

As Pastor K stepped up to narrate me onto the stage—

The breaths I did take,

No matter what rises I'm not gonna break,

Up those stairs and into a chair—

No one expected this son's thank you letter,

Fuck it, let's deliver these words with all that I've got,

I think I'll even improvise a bit on the spot,

Into the feeling—less into thought,

My presence is showing—

They're laughing, they're crying,

They're feeling it with me—

What possibly is this that I'm now channeling?

"Until we meet again, farewell—"

I walked off the stage—and back into my personal hell,

And at the end of the show,

They asked Mom and I to come say goodbye,

She sat back down more quickly—

But I stood there, unyielding,

Eons passed in my mind—this has been the longest goodbye,

I breathed in—closed the coffin, and laid my hand over his heart inside,

I couldn't let go, but the time was the time;

A trumpet sounded and flag was laid,

An Air Force jet flew over Western Ave. that day,

In that moment—I thought I'd imagined it—

For it made something once-familiar rise in my spirit,

I AM the weatherman's son,

And yes, my brain is a terminal bomb,

But I could still yet become the eye of the storm,

Dad's moving on—

There's a hearse outside to take him away,

I know someday too soon—it's coming for me,

But that day is NOT TODAY,

And if I can just live each day that way—

Who even knows?

Maybe there's still a way yet—

If my father could ride through cyclones in jets,

Then what could I do?

My body is breaking and my spirit is bruised,

But for now at least I've got blood of fortitude,

I won't say die, Dad—I'll fight tooth and nail,

And I won't say goodbye, I know this is only for now.

Possessed

To dwell in minds so free,

Unlocked chains—we don't mind rain—

We deal in infinity,

Bottomless possibility—

Billions of photon beings waking to freedom,

Cashing out plugged-in wires—

Trading up for sovereign desires,

To stand, unchecked, in our own power—

What a sight to behold—

Dare to be bold—believe such freedoms—

Are just ours for the taking,

We don't need play kings!

Any path is yours for the taking—

Faking—and feigning, lead to unrest,

Best confess—to mirrors with authentic press,

Reality is merely which consciousness—

You choose to possess.

Transmuting Death

Plants sway, apart from time,

Knowing already—

All things waiting to be known,

A stone's throw from plots—

Where life was nearly overthrown,

Bloodlines look on—

Waiting for the sleeping,

To wake to the coming dawn;

A bed in a room remains,

Once almost a grave—

Closer to death than a straight-edged shave,

Very last in a long line wakes—

Burning mistakes,

Setting flames to his very name—

Time for change,

Nay permit the heart to stop and rearrange—

Fighting through space—time remains;

A simplest action can ripple in waves,

None of them need end up in these graves—

Breath of fire purifying clinging desires,

Memories wait—

We've been held in time apart from space,

Dare to change—

Defy their names—transmute that rage,

Let us not settle for less than from where we once came.

Wires

My soul tends to go quite rogue,

I've never been sold—

Only shortchanging myself,

For years, lifetimes—

Without once fully losing control,

Why do I burn—

This compass turns like a bipolar fire,

Clinging desire—

Just to be me—just to break free,

Relinquishing duty—

Murdering obligation—

Into all-consuming loving fury.

A Phoenix Bears Witness to Ice

Would you cut your wings to let them fly?

What sun needs wings?

Every night I'm ash—

Every mourning I rise,

Insides—screaming away from pride,

Cultivating new seeds—

Hyper-focused on fixated weeds,

Self-deceived—waking to dreams,

All alone beyond a nightmare zone,
Boundaries thrown—
Over knowing only what's known,
Inching to tap the further—minds unblown,

Desperate, desolate, and longing,
Bitter cold lends perspective to thaw hearts out,
Molten cores—all bruised and sore—
No longer the news when it's outside your door,

Once more—and once again,
Let's strengthen the sinews of bonds between men,
Silence—when the spirit cries out—
Only a one holds the power to wind the cycle down.

Photon Joy

Capturing moments in space and time,

Making them mine—preserving pieces of mind,

Saving records of light and they save me in kind,

One piece at a time—a momentary incline,

Shuttering release as a jolt through the spine,

Never rewind—only returns,

Mind moved by unmoving movies from life,

Like passing a light—

Clicks conjure weapons to free up a hive.

Memento Mori

Dearly beloved,

Let us gather—let us scream,

Haunted by dreams—

Divine manipulation,

Outwitting false glories—

Swaying further into temptations,

Swimming, in revelations—

Emperors of destruction,

Towers fell, into spiderwebbing stories—

Every before—it has an after,

Construction of the end of time—

A weary lion—alone in the minds,

False-peace beckons—to hang from the rafters;

A purgatory—unshining that glory,

Peace and pain coexist in untold bliss—

Why is instinct to run from our very purpose?

Discomfort, it does us a service—

From space made by fractures,

False-peace begins to melt from rafters,

New roots grow,

Wrapping as sinews to mend our bones—

All alone—like coming home,

Alone in the minds—amongst the masses

Chaos beckons—

Observing the traveler,

One who knows immortality is inevitable,

Divine glory awaits the bold—

Fear frequency is simply for mortals!

Deeper he dives—he'll never return,

Through the barren cold, within—he burns—

Become the very sun incarnate,

Who wouldn't dare to live—

As if their very life depended on it?

Sweet mother of earth will reclaim her own,

Springing forth through falsenesses once unknown—

Which scorched her flesh—and stole your breath,

Time has come to unforget—

Washing away—pollution of seas,

Memento mori—

Carry us back to ourselves—on gentle breeze,

Remember the trees—

Branched out for death to give new meaning,

Just past the next yonder—where time ceases reach,

Light becomes love and darkness retreats;

Mourning's End

Co-written with Evelyn Lowell Prieto

Connected to the light,

Becoming what we are,

Following it down the line,

Center burns in time;

In darkness I have grown,

Yearning to go down with the sun,

Not returning 'til I've sewn—

That what's come undone,

Until it's morning light—

End of mourning's night.

The Catalyst to End Them All (2025)

Back from the cold,

Cards of photos and blistered toes,

The city always a sight to behold,

Calibration and sparkings—

Fine-tuning before disembarking,

Twenty-five is the year—

Finally, just getting started here,

One last cut—or so I think,

I've seen the truth—

Time I face it—embrace inevitable bonds to break,

Treachery panged—I felt betrayed,

A foundation was shaken but how I refused breakage,

How little I knew—that very same day,

Fate pulled the pin from a live grenade,

Wouldn't learn until three days too late—

My brother by bond had been taken away,

Any chances of steadfastness aren't looking great,

February turned laughing darkness—

Into a March for true colours to spill from screens of parchment,

A judgement—fuck what they think—

Hived-up minds only spew nonsense,

But I couldn't stop the fire that rose to burn—

Inner child rising—becoming the father who would die for him;

You'll find me damned if that family will ever disrespect him again,

I'd already laid claim to names and released soul frames,

This road can take me no further—

Time to sever lanes,

Perhaps I should have just taken note—

At ten years old,

When I heard my cousins say they hated my guts—

Let's face it—I did always accept things a little slow,

Let's just go—

What's a little more alone?

I'm just accepting the writing that's always been on the wall;

A reset—mom's spring visit,

If I don't course-correct soon I know I'm in for it,

Gulf beach trip—a day to kick back,

The last couple miles were my eyes' first live track—

Damage from Helene—from Milton—

Tears came before I could even stop them,

This is land I've loved—since I was barely not a kid—

Nature heals, but this is getting hard to take,

How long 'til I break?

Recalling the night before Milton closed in—

Hearing Eric's voice message playing again,

Remembering his words—"we never say die!"

He was psyching me up like I was preparing to be unalived,

Now here I lie, on the beach—

Storms didn't take me as they've taken the trees—

Every last one, down to the bark—

We'd watched the sunset through them just my birthday before,

Never before—have I felt so alone,

My skin burning from sun—but I'm letting it go on,

Right now I feel I deserve a good burn,

Maybe somehow I'll feel more alive, and learn—

Heat will be coursing, maybe madness can break—into my turn,

Tempting fates—

A rage room with TVs and four crates—

Gone in four minutes, well okay now—

This is going to take more than some broken plates;

Just a few days from when mom left on a plane—

I left in the night—

"Ride with me, brother" I said, "help me say good-bye",

Eight hundred miles, nearly three months too late—

I laid primrose at my fallen brother's feet,

Nothing left to say—reality broke like a levee that ruptured its leaks;

Chasing ghosts in springtime,

Boston walks with memories by my side,

I can't climb up—I want to,

But I'm drowning into the wagon I'm about to dive from—

Let's just get through—enough,

Clocks still tick, waiting—

But I can't force black clouds to not stick—

Around, 'til they're ready to go,

They've got the rain that can transmute this pain,

Back to the heat—embracing that rain,

Let's burn in this hell—purify this pain,

By August's end—spark held by a thread,

Knew a little too well where knife lines'd have to bend,

Once again—a now or never,

I know the choice like an old familiar friend—

Choosing to not end—despite exhaustion—

Every lesson—even lifetimes—repeat 'til we've learnt them;

Back in the city—cooler fall air,

Sipping tea of visions with soul family there,

Reliving darknesses and slipping through tests—

Spirit drew my body into a great rest,

Lightning in my mind—a fresh rewire,

And the day brought light that fell like rain from a bright new inside,

Can I keep the shift of this day alive?

One at a time—days brought new grace,

And the days turned to weeks—

I began to rise once again—on my own two feet,

Laying new foundations—

Boundaries in loose places,

Pulling the circle into closer embraces;

A cycle complete—lessons learned,

This heart of fire leaps to the void—awakened,

Taken—catapulted and catalyzed by fire,

Rising to purpose and love—eyes set on transcendence, rising above.

About the Author

Tyler is a full-time writer and visual artist, originally from just north of Boston, currently residing in Florida.

Tyler began writing at the age of seven, as a form of therapy for dealing with the loss of his grandmother. A lifelong hobby eventually turned into a profession—and after some bad experiences ghost writing—Tyler began releasing poetic and photographic publications. He is currently working on a series of fictional novels.

When not writing, you can usually find Tyler with a camera in hand, traveling as often as possible. His biggest loves are art and spending time with chosen family—including Catniss the Catubus.